Arcadia

Poetry From A Sexual Abuse Survivor

I0103333

John Ryan

chipmunkapublishing
the mental health publisher

John Ryan

Published by
Chipmunkapublishing
PO Box 6872
Brentwood
Essex CM13 1ZT
United Kingdom

http://www.chipmunkapublishing.com

ISBN   978-1-84991-407-9

Cover image by PMK

Chipmunkapublishing   gratefully   acknowledge   the support of Arts Council England.

ABOUT THE AUTHOR

Born in Cappamore, Co. Limerick, Ireland, in 1947, John has experienced mental health issues and been through the system, since a savage sexual assault in the workplace 6 years ago. One thing's for sure: writing was the one constant in an otherwise very inconstant series of experiences; John found the discipline of writing to be very therapeutic indeed, and is writing to this day.

John Ryan

LOVE POEM

Straining the mind to find the right words,
Straining the eyes to catch sight of the birds
Twittering high above on the branch for me
- They symbolise my undying love for thee.

I love the way they fly free in the sky:
My love for thee will always fly high;
There's just you and me in our little love-nest:
We fly in our love where love is the best.

Oh! come let us fly in the morn' and at noon
Oh' come let us fly by the light of the moon;
Like swallows we'll fly and catch all the flies
- Like swallows we'll know every inch of the skies.

And when we are tired we'll fly yet again
For now we are free, our wings take the strain;
Oh! come, my sweet lovely, fly low and fly high:
The earth is all ours, and so is the sky.

Oh! come now, my lovely, my love is for thee,
When we are together it is then we are free:
Let's fly by day and again by night
- Together we make a beautiful sight.

FULL MOON

Last night I stared, and stared again,
The full moon stared back down;
I stared upon its happy face,
It took away my frown.

For I was sure besotted now,
Transfix'd by my sweet moon:
My song I sang in innocence,
My moon sang back in tune.

By now we both were intertwined,
Caught in mystic ruse;
My moon and I forever one
- We shall forever fuse.

Oh! mystic orb, my damsel sweet,
Come stare with me tonight,
For I shall wait, and wait for thee,
For such a comely sight.

Forever we shall be as one,
Forever share thy light;
The day is all too long to wait,
Oh!come, my sacred night.

SILENCE

I visit Silence often:
Silence visits me, too.
We are the best of friends.

A fine spring morning, and
We are walking together,
Communing together,
Exchanging words together.

We know our mutual moods,
We know each other's needs.
We block out so much reality
To obtain a great degree of
Concentration.

And that brings great, great
Peace. And yet, yet sometimes,
Great, great pain. Silence:she
Demands, demands, no less, an
Absolute commitment to her
Friendship, no ifs , no buts.

Superficially, it looks an odd
Set-up. The reality is a mutually-
Advantageous relationship, full
Of joys beyond words.

I'M WRITING NOW

I'm writing now with diligence:
The Muse beside me still,
For I have spent these past few hours
Wasting time until

Originality came forth,
The spark of something new;
Picking words to tell my tale,
The Muse and I make two

Strong minds who savour faultless script,
Who delight in stirring rhyme;
So often we had disagreed
- We've got it right this time.

And when I think it's all been done
To perfection, oh! such rage!
I see the imperfections glare
At me from off the page!

My Muse, do guide me in my quest,
Grant me light to see
Thy gift of script ephemeral
-And then I'll happy be.

A BIT OF WISDOM

For always there will be a time, recalling
Happy times of yore, innocence now made
Bold, more so, as Age tightens its grip.

For always there will be a time to wish that
Nature would hold off its imposition of
Degenerating poise: 62's not 26, time
Takes its toll.

For always there will be a time to mourn a;;
The things we lose through time, to touch the
Powd'ry bricks of ancient towns: others' loss
A gain for us.

For always there will be a time to watch and
Stare as roses bloom, to see the moon ride
Out the storm on wintry nights, ploughing
Her way through milky clouds.

For always there will be a time to be oneself,
Defying all predictions, and growing old -
Gracefully.

I AM A ROSE

I am a rose beyond compare,
Spreading sweet smells in a
World polluted, almost
Beyond redemption.

I can measure my blooms in
Days, weeks: they judge me
Not when I am dead-headed.
They know what I have yet
To give.

The older I am, the better
The blooms - some say the
Sweeter the scent. My
Secrets I hold within, deep
Deep inside.

My gnarled, skeletal form
Betrays the beauty still to
Give:but will they cut me
Back and cosset me the
Better to withstand the

Winter's rattling 'gainst the
Window pane, in howling
Frosty gale? In winter I'm
Alone, forgotten as the
Snow piles up, nature's

Juices deep preserved for
Summer's show, and full
Delight for all. Feed me in
The Spring and I will more
Than give my all as blooms

Arcadia

They multiply in summer's
Heat: I give my all in silent
Wafts of scent: that is my
Joy. I bring a smile to faces
Ravaged by the winter's

Wind. My roots are deep
And full of nourishment:
Don't judge me by my
Knarled form, but by my
Scented summer's blooms.

John Ryan

THE EMPTY PAGE

I came upon this white page all alone
And crying out to be covered-up.

"I came into the world naked: it is my
Destiny to be filled; indeed, I shall spend
Eternity wandering the Land of the Unfilled
Should it be that nobody fills me with words
- Fine words, positive words, ennobling
Words".

My heart took pity on the empty page, and
I began to lovingly cover it with words, the
Kind of words which would grant it the
Freedom it craved.

SECTIONED

A friend of a friend is "Sectioned"
Under the Mental Health Act:
A way of life imposed, what was
No longer is: what is, is born of
Desolate grief. What will be, will be
For the foreseeable future.

My memories are raw.

Loss of sleep, of appetite, of the
Will to live, on suicide watch.
Being looked-at, gaped-at,

Avoiding eye-to-eye response,
At any cost. So disconcerting,
And Society, to top it all, is
So suspicious.

John Ryan

A FIELD AFAR

I'm thinking of a field afar:
Consecrated ground in Ireland
Where my sister lies in peace.
Ne'er we'll forget the happy hours
In happy times in Faery fields
Playing as kids play in innocence.
This field is now the bond
Between the living and the dead;
The grave a final resting-place in peace.
Gentle, misty Irish rain sprinkles down
As if from heav'n itself: are you aware
Of this, my sister dear? Do you see us
Gathered here, and does our presence
Make a difference? To us it does,
I simply ask if it makes a difference
To you - knowing, as you do, our love
And deep respect this passing hour?

THE WORLD HAS GONE TO WORK

The world has gone to work,
But I've been up since dawn,
Beavering away at words, and
Bits of words, old words, new
Words. I force myself to
Compose, lest I lose the knack.

Yesterday's ease is today's
Impossibility. But it will pass.

I muse upon the vagaries of
Old age. I'm slowing up. My
Flowers and my garden
Cheer me up no end. But
Words elude me now, the
Wisdom of the Ages is for
Nought, it seems.

For now, at least.

John Ryan

MEDITATION

That moody, sombre time before the winter's
Wasted ways, a time of soberness indeed,
A time to think alone of those we miss so much
In death. But not disconsolate. For their lives
Mean so much more than the fact of leaving
As they did, so silently and dignified.

That happy time: for happiness is what they
Gave, and give, this precious hour, the memory
Of happy hours of shared delight.

And as I walk with stick in hand, I tread so gently
On the leaves of ev'ry colour, hue: each one a
Testament to Nature's ways, one for each good
Soul now passed away this year.

Oh! come my Muse and share with me this thoughtful
Hour, and we will dwell for e'er upon the memory
Of those souls we miss so much. But not so sadly as
To miss the point of Life: we treasure happy
Thoughts abd happy times in happy mood,
Positive in all our thoughts, for that is what they'd want.

INSPIRATION

I climbed a hill and still no success
In creating a new poem, for the
Muses are far away this hour, so I
Clambered back down - dejected.

I climbed the hill again, and pleaded
With the gods that, this time, an
Angry mind might be placated, such
As would pen the words that please
The gods themselves.

Alas! I am afraid that I have lost the
Precious gift: perchance the Muses
Take this gift and give it to another
Who will, instead of me, become a
Favourite of the gods. I clambered
Back down - dejected.

Yet again I climbed the hill, and in
Weakening voice I shouted to the
Muses to see my work in former
Times, and lo! I felt the spark of
Olden times and happy times and
Times when we communed in
Selfless ways to please the gods.

No more clambering down,
Dejected, for now I have the
Precious gift of eloquence
Again, and all is happy now
Once more atop my precious
Hill.The spring was flowing,
I slaked my thirst and now
I felt the urge to write to
Please the Muses
And the gods combined.

John Ryan

I SLEEP SO MUCH IN WINTERTIME

I sleep so much in wintertime,
I sleep so much in tune
With nature's rhythm in wintertime,
I'll hibernate quite soon.

Sleepy season, sleepy time
When all of nature's dead;
I sleep along with nature,
The Book of Sleep I've read.

Oh! let me sleep, and sleep again,
Hibernate, I plead,
For sleep is all I want this time
- Just let me keep my sleep.

I want to wake in springtime,
Refreshed and full of life;
Behind me death and all such things -
behind me all such strife.

ROSES

I love it when the roses bloom,
When all the colours are on show;
When in their majesty they bow,
- For they'll have withered much too soon.

The summer months, oh! how they fly
Leaving us in tender peace,
Would that this show would never cease
- Instead of which I start to cry.

Winter's winds loom just ahead,
My wonderful display will cease
And I will lose my sense of peace
- Soon all these roses will be dead.

My garden will be spare and tight,
My roses will be gone for e'er;
Come winter with its freezing layer
- My garden will lose all its light.

I love it when the roses bloom,
My memories help to keep me bright;
But now we're losing all the light:
Alas! they've withered all too soon.

John Ryan

THE SWALLOWS ALL HAVE FLOWN

The swallows all have flown,
And I am left to mourn their loss.
I'll miss the acrobatic dance, the
Aerial ballet just for me. Such
Pleasure now will be no more,
Alas.

Yet all's not doom and
Gloom: when much else is
Forgot', the memory
Will force a smile.

No more the cuckoo's
Muffled call - she, too, has
Sped to warmer climes. A
Memory to cherish, sure,
When winter's grip has
Left its mark.

I miss them all this lonesome
Hour, the chirping opera
Stars who gave their all just
So I'd hear on balmy summer
Days. My pleasures now
Indoors, the gladiolas in full
Bloom in my sitting-room.
Glad I had a summer just like
This, to be repeated next
Time round - we hope.

THE RAIN

The rain is pelting on the window hard,
And I can hear the wind throughout the house;
An hour ago, the sun it brightly shone
- All so quiet, one could hear a mouse.

The change it came so suddenly,
The wind came up so quiet,
The dazzling sun then disappeared
And lo! We lost the light.

It makes me think of life's strange ways,
The way things come to pass,
And I am here so all alone
- The raindrops fall en masse.

They press against the window pane,
And dance in rivers down:
My former visage, happy, bright,
Is replaced now with a frown.

And yet, as I do pen these words,
The blue sky distant shows;
The garden's got a sprinkling
- So did my favourite rose.

COME TO ME AND TELL ME NOW

Come to me and tell me now of olden times
When we were young and asking no Big Questions.
For now I'm old and want to share those days
Of innocence and carefree times, when we did wander
Faery fields and country lanes, and life was so, so full
Of skitty laughter 'midst the summer growth.
Oh! come to me and tell me more, and I'll forever
Happy be, with all my pains and aches dissolved.
October now: that time to think and think again,
Fill my life with happiness, let mem'ries flood my days
And I'll for e'er be free.

A NEW DAY

The night is coming to a close:
Dawn announces day's arrival
Imperceptibly. It pulls back the
Curtains on a new day.
The lights go out, and now
There is the miracle of sudden sight.
The sun is up, the air is crisp:
Nature waits for no one.
The sodden cobweb trembles
In the breeze: a multi-coloured
Miracle all ablaze in sharp sunlight,
Quivering to greet the day.
Who's to say what this day will bring?
Does it bode for good or ill?
Either way, I'm happy here,
To greet the dawn, as my Muse departs
To Faery fields afar.

MID-SEPTEMBER

My favourite chestnuts show signs of wear,
Still delightful, but worn. So, so quiet this
Early morn', a gentle breeze wafts through
These leaves, swaying gently to and fro.

The sharp cold: the first intimations of colder
Times ahead. The nights are darker earlier,
My summer now is o'er, a move to meditation
And to introspection - but not just yet.

That time between delightful summer and
All it meant, and the severity of winter-time,
Preparing for that winter time, but still
Delightful days with lots of sunshine to ingest

A feel of sheer delight within. My walks already
Are so different: my thoughts not so exuberant.
But Beauty stalks the woods and trees: I just
Need eyes to see, and mind to penetrate.

A crisp September morn', all so quiet and peaceful
Now. The rush-hour it has passed, and my time
Has come to walk about, smell the smells and scent
The scents that September has to offer me this hour.

HEATHROW DEPARTURE

Groaning under the weight, the Jumbo
Passes overhead on its way to
God-knows-where: who is to say what
Emotions are tied-up in its belly?
Anticipation, despair, and everything
In-between?

There is no going-back now.
It is committed.

And so with my day: I am up, writing
And forever sensitive to the needs of
The day ahead: no going-back now.

As I gaze across the sky I see those arriving:
The sky over London hums with the
Procession of those both leaving and arriving.
Countless human emotions
Contained within the glamour of those noisy
Capsules, a tide of humanity on the move to
Even newer emotions. Without respite.

No going-back now, either way . . .

John Ryan

AN HOUR OF QUIETNESS

An hour of quietness alone
'Midst flaming flowers,

My city garden looks so neat,
affords me great delight.

The scent from roses fills my
Nose, and all is happy here

This August hour. Would that
The world could join me in my

Hour of joy.

AND THERE WERE TIMES

And there were times when we would
Sit and nothing say, and they were
Precious times indeed, for love was
Warm, relaxed, not needing to
Repeat itself.

But now the gulf of death, the hope
That we will meet again, for that is
All that's left to me this sad, sad hour
Alone.

The gnawing ache of grief, long-term.
The urge to get away, forget. And when
We do, Grief greets us in our new-found
Place of grief.

THE DREAM

For I would love to dream
The dream of dreams,
The dream to crown them all;
All my friends would be there
Happy, cheerful, the way
The dream of dreams would
Have it.

Happy to replace the nightmare
All so common: happy to
Replace the half-dreams, not
So happy, cheerful, the way
With half-dreams.

For I would love to dream all
Night and dream again that
All is well with friends who
Last the test of time.

THE TREE

The big, big tree next door
Is restless, such a delight
To see it in action, I'm
Rooted to the spot,
Absorbed.

It's relishing the wind,
The August wind,
The warm Westerly.

I'm rejuvenated,
Just watching,
Observing, and
Becoming
One with
The tree.

EAST FINCHLEY

I went down the High Road
And met my Muse quite by
Chance: we went to
Cherry Tree Woods, where
We conversed under the
Trees and watched the
Squirrels dart about.

I turned to gaze once more
At my guest and lo! she was
Gone - vanished.

DOZING

I am dozing in my garden of delights,
It's September and the roses are
Triumphant, staring me, wondering if
I will sniff and wallow in the scent. I'm
into Mahon deep this fine and goodly
Hour. The spotless blue above, the
Multicoloured roses next to me combine
To make my pleasure total. The Muses
Hover round about, the gods they smile
As well, and I am true content: this state
Of bliss will never last, I whisper to my
Muse. But while it does I copy busy bees
And store for future times the secrets
Learnt from Mahon and his like. My Muse,
Stay with me in this bower and teach me
Secrets more, for all too soon the
Inspiration it will pass, and I'll be left alone.

RETURNING

I wish to go back there, the place where I grew up,
Spend some time walking the lanes and byways so,
So familiar to my memory.

Sixty years have changed the place: the world has
Moved on. So have I. The world has been busy
Adapting - so have I, sometimes feverishly so.

And yet, the trees and stones remember me, and
I remember them so well; and when I went I
Couldn't find the trees and stones, perhaps my
Age is telling now.

Though the Muse was with me, all was silent and
Had changed: I knew it would before I went. Yet
The need was there to go and see what nature
Left for such as me.

My lot is there to be interpreted anew, romantic
Notions are for other times and places, essential
Bits are missing this dire day, and still I love
Dromsally, Cappamore: for that is who I am.

THE PLOUGH

The rusty plough is smothered by the nettles
Tight, Nature holds its own, ensures that none
Will come too near as this master of design is
Laid to rest, its lifetime journey now complete.
Who is to say what stories it could tell as it
Broke new ground in its heyday now long gone?
Bulky, heavy, impossible to manoeuvre by
Itself; once pulled, it slewed along defying
Gravity and cut a straight line with finesse,
Revealing secrets from the soil, picked
Eagerly by birds from God-knows-where.
But now abandoned, left to rust, open to
The elements, its secrets still intact, held
Within the changing hue as one more shower
Drenches it anew. Specks of multicoloured
Metal gleam in midday sun, and a frosty layer
Of icing makes it come to life once more. So
Many folk will pass it by, and give it not a thought,
Yet within its frame so skeletal we have a moral
Of what life could be through Ages of Mankind.

NIGHT FLIGHT

From my bedroom window I stare at the
Street-lamp: two-thirty and everything is
Dead - the world has gone to sleep.

But not so.

The midgets are swarming around the
Lamp, performing acrobatics round the
Orange glow. The regular fox scowls his
Way, tail up, on his regular prowl.

The local cat scurries under a car. And
Who's to say what creepy-crawlies are
Busy on the night-shift, unseen, unheard?
Cobweb-time. And who's to say if Muses
Flit the Spheres in search of souls like me,
This darkened hour?

Night flight, indeed.

SHOCK NEWS

And I could think of other times
When life was sure, no questions
Asked, and then the news came
Through that you were dead.

If only we had one more time to
Laugh, one more time to share
A moment of sheer doubt, but
No, 'twas not to be, alas.

I bear my burden with some
Grace but , truth be told, I miss
You terribly. I miss the way you
Looked at me, and smiled at me

First thing, and all the other
Things that made you who you
Were. For I did love the times,
The happy times, the times when

We would share a thought and
Laugh and laugh again, when you
Would visit me at home, and share
Together all I had, little though it was

For a soul as kind as you, dear Anne.
My soul is unconsolable this hour, my
Dear, dear sister sweet. But I am happy
To have had a sister just like you.

John Ryan

THE PSYCHIATRIC WARD

I remember my days in the psychiatric ward,
I look back without fear or dread. Now I am
Much improved, enjoying life and every bit
Of it. A far cry from those October days. How
Life changes: then, we feared for life itself,
Now we fear losing the zest for life.

Inevitably, autumn is remembrance time, the
Fall from sanity itself. As I then gazed at
The trees, I loved every moment, the sheer
Colour and scale of movement as a myriad
Leaves fell and graced the ground. A happy
Interlude.

Those leaves,multi-coloured and of such
Delicacy, now long-forgotten: even in freefall
They offered such delight in those unhappy
Days. I painted them with such exquisite care.
My one and only source of delight in an abysmal
Situation. Who could compose exquisite poetry
In such conditions?

And yet, the Spirit survived and survives to this hour.
Perhaps my Muse will take pity . . .

PLAY TIME

Across the road are two enormous
Horse-chestnuts, noble and resilient;
It's September, and the outer edges
Touch. The individual leaves play
Acrobatic games in the stiff but
Pleasant wind.

Rare creatures in a city setting. And
So silent through the summer, but
Any day now the winds of autumn
Will make their conversations
Audible. Their absence would make
A terrible cut in the local landscape.

Their architectural form is a
Meditation in itself: and so humble,
Given that they will outlive us all.

SEPTEMBER RAIN

The first rains of autumn.
After a delightful summer,
A sudden reminder of
The old ways.

Though everything is soaking,
The rain is gentle and soft,
And now intermittent.

My walking-stick fails to get
A grip on the slithery
surface.

A contemplating
Crow rides out the mist,
Motionless on its perch.

All the smaller birds have
Taken cover long ago. So
Have most humans.
Not me:
I'm enjoying my walk.

AFTERNOON SILENCE

I sit and listen in the silence of the afternoon,
Surrounded by books that cry out to be read.
Books crave attention, have an insatiable need
To be held and fondled. I enjoy the sheer
Physicality of the written word in my hands.
And always the silence, my loving companion.

My Muse is drawn to the silence, too. There is
The distant hum of traffic on the High Road.
That alone is enough to scare my Muse away.
Silence, like the books so loved, demands
Cosseting, and disappears if neglected. So
Fortunate to live where I do, and to live the
Way I do, 'midst Silence sweet.

ROSES FOR COMPANY

I am thinking quietly
With my roses for company:
No monochrome scene this.
The cat from down the road
Is here. The pleasure from
Stroking, aided by purrs of
Encouragement, is
Beyond words.

My roses are putting-on a last
Display before settling-in for the
Long, long winter sleep.
I feel so attached to them,
And know every fold and
Blossom.

Thank goodness for roses, for cats,
For my time to muse with my Muse.

TORUN

(University city in northern Poland)

For I loved the time when we were there
In Poland, wandering through Torun's
Giddy architecture. And we were right:
They came from all over, young and old,
To see Copernicus on his pedestal, to
See the well-preserved sense of place
And time this warm spring day.

For I loved the time we spent at Babcia's
Grave, the flowers and votive lamps a
Testament to love enduring still. The
Dove appeared upon the window-sill
and then flew on, having gazed on us
And made us wonder still if we were
Meant to read the runes aright. Did
Babcia want us all to know that all was
Well with her? Or was it just coincidence?

For I loved the time we spent at Bashia's
Plot and saw the handiwork of one who
Loved the trees and flowers, and
Vegetables, too. Devoted to an ordered
Life, it made me think, and think again.

For I loved the very sense of place this
Springtime hour, for we were here
Relaxed, and met old friends and
Kissed the babies and the relatives with
Passion undiminished. This was Poland
At its very best, the churches and the
Public buildings, architectural
Splendours shouting out their wares
- If only we could see, and see again.

But see we did, and gaped and stared
At visual delights: who could pass and
Not look up, make mental notes of all
There was to see? Besotted we became,
For detail followed detail, but in complete
Harmony.

For I loved the time when Chopin's music
Came to mind, and this little piece of
Europe made us feel so good.

To Babcia

I loved the way you smiled and joked
When times were good, and death ten
Thousand miles away, we never, even
Then, thought you'd be gone from us
This day. The shock of seeing you
Laid in state, the shock, the shock.

For you were made to joke and smile
As only you could do. We still love
You now, in death, that smile still on
Your face this day. The shock of
Seeing you laid in state,
The shock, the shock.

We couldn't bring ourselves to think
That here you would be laid, for
Life was good and humorous.
That said, we never thought of
Death so near, the shock of
Seeing you laid in state,
The shock, the shock.

John Ryan

DAFFODILS

The delicate sprawl of yellow
And white silently trumpeting
The arrival of spring. Bobbing
About in the April wind, and
Sunshine, they attest to the
End of a long, long wait:
Spring is here and Easter's
On the way. Bright mornings,
Long evenings, 'tis springtime
Now for sure. A new-found
Pace in the step, a longing
Gasp for summer air. Bulbs
Planted deep in autumn's
Gloom announce the end
Of winter's grip, and we can
See ahead to brighter days.
The sheer delight of watching
Nature take a bow, while
Daffodils smile their smile of
Hope, and dance their routine
With wild abandon.

AFTERNOON NAP

I sleep the sleep of angels soft,
Until the doorbell rings,
The springtime sunshine filters
Through the curtains crisp

And there I am, breathing like
A babe, dreaming as the angels
Dream. Alternate world, soft
And safe, yet so until the
Doorbell brings it to an end
Without apology.

The gods look on, and maybe
Smile (who knows?) maybe
Not, for reality catches
Sleepers unawares.

A warning shot, perhaps lest
Sleep hold sleepers captive in
The springtime sun. A sense
That sleep and wakefulness
Fight battles for the soul of
Such as me. Ignore the bell,
Sleep on and sleep the sleep
That angels sleep.

MY BOOK OF POEMS

My book of poems,
My book of joy,
- My book of sorrow,
Too, my source of
Insight through the
Moon-lit hours.
Inspiration looms
Within a stony breast
And yet evaporates
Again: my book of
Poems rekindles all
Once more. My wordy
Friend berates me for
My lassitude, my book
Befriends me in my
Hour of need. The
Smell of pages new
- and old - is pure
Delight: my book of
Joy and sorrow
Serves me well, so
Well, in fact, that I
No longer am
Aggrieved this hour,
This goodly hour of
Night.

LAMENT

I miss you, Anne,
gentle that you were
to me: good friends.

Obsessed about your
whereabouts these
days: yet I know your
Time's not measured
like to ours.

Hungry just to catch a
glimpse once more,
share a smile, a
recognition of those
times we were
together then.

Who suspected you'd
be gone, and all too soon?
Not me.
Not me.

BEYOND THE GRAVE

If only we knew what reality lies
Beyond the grave: we could
Take the measure of life,
Fine-woven.

If only we knew what reality lies
This side of the grave: there lies
The rub.

If only we could listen-in on the
Conversations of angels, indeed
On the replies of our loved ones.

If only we could converse with
Them.

If only we had a mere glimpse of
The reality beyond the grave . . .

THE POSTMAN

Waiting patiently for the postman to
Arrive, I sit and think of what these
Books of poems might contain, for I
Need nourishment inside my mind.

And yet I know precisely what's in
Store this time, and simply cannot
Wait to wallow in the pleasure of a
Read, my fuel for soul and mind.

There goes the bell, the postman at
The door, the bringer of good tidings
This fine spring morning hour. Delight
Within my breast, the famine o'er.

And I will gorge myself and smell the
Books, newly-minted, waiting now to
Be handled like a new-born babe, so
Full of potential for my famished mind.

DILEMMA

So much passion,
Locked-up in a few brief words:
Can reason and passion ever be
Equated? Can a reasonable,
Compassionate compromise
Ever be found, such that we
Can get-on with life?

COCKCROW COMPOSITION

Staring at my page, I wonder what can
justify such labour and such patience
now; the urge to share has taken over
all my conscious senses this waking,
springtime morn'. Distractions play
their wily games, so early in the day.

Nature's in-built prod to write is
overcome so easily, I plod along and
hope that I can stay awake, kept
company by cockerels denoting all is
new and fresh, and crisp and
gloating joyously for wretched souls
like me.

On and on they cry, repeating the
refrain heard a thousand years ago.
Close-up, as if the first time ever,:me,
too, at my empty page.

Lonely cockerel, lonely scribe:
we make a perfect match.

John Ryan

MARCH MEDITATION

Cool March morning, pleasant in the crispy air,
And still I want to commune deep with Muses
As I pace myself for future walks with meditative
Gait. Let's commune this sheltered hour, let us
See what lies in wait for favourites of the gods -
Pride before a fall, maybe, but a fervent hope
Within the breast that inspiration may this time
Be held in gentle arms. Distractions crowd around,
City noise holds hostage all the good intent built-up
Through time, evaporating graces freely given and
Gratefully received. But on I tread, slowly making
Progress here, slowly making progress there, a
Sense that somehow spring may come quite soon
To souls so starved of sunshine in the soul.

TO MY DEAD SISTER

We buried you with full honours
And yet I want to have one last
hug, one last chance to share
the times we missed together.

You were there and I was here,
Now you are There and I am here:
still pining for the times together
when we simply loved to laugh
and laugh again - gently, as only
you were gentle in your laugh.

The pain, the pain of grief, the
times that might have been
when we'd have shared so
much, and yet I know that I
will wail in vain, for you won't
be coming back to me . . .

We live on in wanton hope that
one day all will be revealed, and
we will share a brighter day where
darkened clouds will all be cleared
and, reunited, the music from the
valley rising through the ether far,
will be our mutual epitaph.

STILL-BIRTH

The poem died at birth,
It didn't stand a chance:
Ill-conceived, and starved
Of thought from the outset.
The poem grew within my
Soul for all this time, until
The pain was unbearable.
I'd thought the time had
Come, yet deep within I
Knew there wasn't
Something right. My Muse
Had been, but suddenly
Withdrew. Alone, I mourn
The loss, alone I screw the
Paper up, and dump it in
The bin, in mourning all
I do is stare, exhausted . . .

SUDDEN DEATH

She visits only once
And when she does
The shock is all too
Palpable.

So swift, so silent.
She creeps with
Stealth, and snaps
Our health.

A sudden dart of
Recognition: things
Will be no more: a
Sharp intake of breath.

Stunned, we try to
Take it in, but all
We do is brood
In disbelief.

The shock.

TEMPTATION

Look inside the cover
of this newly-published
book, and all will be
revealed, it said. Poetry
like you've never read
before. And lo! I did
indeed find words of
comfort, warmth and
insight. Words that
felt so true to life, but
disturbed the inner sense
of lazy peace, a solace
quickly gone, alas. Misty
words that made no peace,
and yet I read and read and
chewed the cud till time
itself cut me short. Tempted
still to catch a glimpse of future
lines, always tempted toward
the future in one mad rush of
eyelid movement, rather than
to swallow the bitter truth that
stares me from the present page.

THE POEM WITHIN

Deep within the breast
lies a secret thought,
a nugget of fine wisdom
anxious to escape. If
only I could catch the
moment now, and
place it on the page
fresh and struggling to
survive. A fervid mind
struggles to create the
pearl of wisdom for a
moment's gift, to hold
a phrase so accurate
before it's lost
for e'er.

John Ryan

REMEMBRANCE TIME

I shuffle through the mounds of leaves
Deliberately, for the hell of it: to hear the
Squelching sound of dry, crisp leaves
Underfoot. This is Remembrance time.

Through the spring and summer these
Very leaves evolved, now will become
So much mulch: earth to earth. The
Cycle is complete, leaf to leaf-mould.

My progress is slow, deliberate, the
Sound underfoot a speciality of autumn.
I'm oblivious to all about, such is the
Childlike sense of abandonment to sound.

SEPTEMBER GALE

Early September, the first
Winds od discontent, a gale this
Early, and yet not cold. The
Heavens are a-moving, re-arranging
The furniture above, the listless
Feel of sultry August suddenly gone.

A shock to the system, accustomed
To languid, lazy days, the whole sky
In turmoil.

And I like it so.

The blooms of roses rare lay
Scattered all about: I dead-head
In the hope that we might get one
More flourish still. Above, a faultless
Bluey sky and all is fresh and crisp
This chirpy, happy hour.

And I like it so.

THE HORSE CHESTNUT

In November, it stands forlorn,
Naked, its main organs exposed
To all who care to notice,
Unable to escape to warmer
Climes. Seeing it in this state
Comes as a shock: we got used to
The canopy of foliage, the
Noble bearing through the
Summer.

Now bereft of dignity, it
Points in all directions as if to
Confuse. And still we gape,
Mesmerised. The raw wind
Makes no impression on its
Nakedness - so it will be until
Spring-time comes again.

I DON'T KNOW

I don't know if I can overcome
that inherent tendency towards
depression. We've tried so many
tactics, and medication, and yet
back it comes, each time stronger
than before. It eats away at
motivation, chewing originality
before it had a chance to
develop. Well-intentioned folk
say Do this, Do that - to no
avail. Back to Zero, facing
my own Ego. Lord, clear this
cloud of manic depression
from my heart.

John Ryan

SUBURBAN WALK

A feverish mind needs a breath of fresh air,
So I stroll up Leslie Road, stick in hand, and
Back down Leopold Road. Twenty minutes
Of delight, as I ruminate and work precisely
The order of the words upon the page.

To some, a lonely occupation, but to me a
Source of pleasure now, as my mind is
Fully occupied, and the sweet, sweet scent
Of Muses near is all too much to bear. Come,
My Muse, and walk with me, and talk with me,
And stir my mind.

For journeys further still with thee. The rain is
Dew-drenched inspiration wild, for now I'm
All inspired to walk for e'er with thee.
Suburban streets don't fright me anymore,
Days long gone, good riddance, too.

Come
My Muse,
Don't
Leave me
Now.

ALONE (2)

All alone, yet full of mental strength
To face the daily grind together with
my poems so uplifting In my soul.
The world says No, don't be alone,
But I say Be alone, and search the
meaning further still. My days ain't
Long enough for projects such as this,
Such is my delight dissembling words
And words and words.

All alone this hour, masticating in my
Lair, giving birth to new-laid forms of
Words that stimulate the appetite for
More, facing up to long-held
Mysteries - hoping that I might be
A newly-minted Me.

THE MUSE HAS FLED

Woe is me, my Muse is gone to ground,
The pain, the pain of separation is too
Much to bear, so deeply do I want to
Pen a piece acceptable to her so Deeply
Do I pain this hour.

Woe is me indeed.

The times they were so plentiful, when
I did lie with her and we penned such
Wordy Musak as to please her so, but
Lo! I cannot even find her, much less
Play wordy games in her embrace.
Woe is me this lonely hour.

Woe is me indeed.

THAT TIME OF YEAR

That time of year again
when things are moving to a close,
and yet we know the very death
of things will be the very life of
things, come spring.

Death is merely a respite, a
passing phase in the wider
scheme of things. All is not
lost, as we once thought.

We concentrate on what will be
- lest we wallow in despair.

I WANT TO BE MYSELF

I want to be myself, quiet, kind and lyrical
- But when I immerse myself in others' work
I somehow want to be them.

I want to have written what they have written.
But no - I must write what I write, then be truly
Me. The influence of others is always calling at
The doorbell: my inner self is harder to detect.

That bell, it rings incessantly, I must know
Myself alone, to know when to refuse to
answer it.

The pain of originality. The sometime ease of
Originality. I want to be myself. The influence
Of others is hard to disregard. but I must be
Me when answering that bell.

I want to be myself.

OLD FRIENDS

I met a friend:
We talked about old times,
It's obvious to me I've changed
To a much more private, poetic
Person, these last few years. I'm
Not sure that's a compliment.
Indeed, I'd say it's verging on
The troublesome. It shows my
Age, not my maturity.
And yet, I'm glad I'm me.

All that was then, this is now:
I'm rooted in my own poetic
Reality, rejecting so, so much in
Favour of a much more private,
Sensitive way of seeing my reality.

ALONE

We are left
with our thoughts
- everything else
has vanished.
Stripped like this
is not pleasant,
until, that is,
we find we cope
alone, and cope
quite well.
Society says we
shouldn't be alone:
necessity demands
we be alone, if
only to confront
our inner selves.
It can be quite
surprising, even
a revelation. The
pain of parting is
amply compensated
for: the joy of
being alone is its
own reward.

AUTUMN EVENING

Autumn evening: ten to six
and dusk arrives, no sooner
here than scampered by
the Dark, for all is short and
brief these days, these days
of brilliant sunshine in the
mor'n, and temperatures
unseasonably high.

Yet I can sense the winter's
envious grasp as
imperceptibly we lose the
very leaves to wintry blasts:
the leaves that make this
precious time precisely what
it is - an interlude, a time to
recollect, before we freeze,
recoil from snowy air
and await out fate for
months to come.

John Ryan

THE URGE TO WRITE

I so much want to write anew,
to punch the empty page with
marks which indicate an inner
pulse. And so, to write or scrawl:
marks which defile and doodle
or marks which lift the spirits
from this mundane life.
Those marks upon the page
are but the end - the
process is within, has come full
term and must disgorge itself
upon the page. Coaxed to
breathe new life, an independent
force for good or ill.
But oh! the pain, and more so for
the sorting here, the shifting
there. These words must breathe
alone not only to survive, but
to mean beyond the norm.
But oh! the pain.

A GRAVE REVISITED

We visit you again this autumn time
weighed down with love and kindness
for the times that were so real and
meaningful; we busy ourselves with
rearranging flowers and votive lamps,
but the silence speaks most eloquent.
In reality we revisit our inner selves:
readjusting to the bolt from the blue
that you were gone from us for e'er.

"Cry not for me" I hear you whisper
through the rustling leaves - one
falls so gently on your grave and
fulfills its destiny as you would have
it so. Our inner selves are weak and
tired from the constant sense of
loss. Faces, contorted now with
pain, the pain of grief, faces staring
at the grave and tears come
gushing forth for old times' sake.

The cruelty of parting gasps, then
one gentle voice remembers now
a happy time and the smothered
laugh is echoed round about.
For we believe that you're aware
of our sense of duty done, complete.
For we believe that you're aware
of our presence here this hour.
For we're aware that all's
complete, and leave, no more
distressed, our task is done,
and we are cleansed within.

NOVEMBER

November time, a time to sleep,
To hibernate the next few hours:
The sweet, white wine of summer sours -
Wintertime is one small leap.

November time, a time of sleep:
Repatriation in the ground;
And then there is no sound,
But lots of memories to keep.

The busy bees, and wild swans found
In foreign parts this time of year;
They've flown afar without a tear -
No more we'll hear their unique sound.

November time, this time recalls
The happy sounds of summer far
Away by now, but hark!
Methinks a deathly pall befalls

On humankind who tell the tale,
Survive and die in November's grip;
Next year the summer wine we'll sip
- Summer's coming without fail.

November time, a time to brood
On life's deep meaning, understood;
On summer's memories, come in a flood,
For winter's pain to sooth.

AUTUMN LEAVES

Leaves, confetti-like, descend
in clusters round about, as the
wind sees fit. They gave pleasure
in their freshness through the
spring, now give pleasure as I
crunch them underfoot. For
autumn is my time: the time
to dwell on cycles old and new,
the time to dwell on multicoloured
mysteries now lain aimlessly about.
The tree denuded of its leaves: was
Nature ever as beautiful as now
they scamper, play about and rush
to time-scales different to our own . . .

John Ryan

EVERYONE WANTS LIFE

Everyone wants life, but what if,
perchance,Life within evaporates?
The pain: that special pain if this
should be a loved one. But love
transcends that special pain,
painful love is all we have,
enough to fill a life of yearning
here and now.

But everyone, and everything,
wants life, and yet, perchance,
I do perceive that death creates
a newer life beyond, that love
transmits its life to lifeless form
just now; for all is life and all is
death , forever intertwined: the
fundamental rule that we may
rue should we forget.

FOR WHEN I DIE

For when I die
don't let me lie
alone: in life I
felt alone, but
never really
wanted it so.

For when I die
keep me in your
thoughts: for in
my life, I often,
often thought
of you, just you.

For when I die
celebrate my
love of life:
my life of love
for none
but thee.

AUTUMN MOON

The milky autumn moon will all
too soon give way to morning's
misty, chilly sun; only lovers
will recall the detail of these
passing hours.

I keep lone
vigil with my love, the Muse:
we are forever bound by pact
enacted on a night like this so
many moons ago.

But oh!
the pain of waiting for
that inspiration to amuse
my Muse. That she'll inspire
my mind this watery night,
and we can play with words
to please the gods beyond.

NOVEMBER TIME

Remembering the quick and dead, November time,
When life is slower still, a hard frost coats the earth,
Our closeness to the dead is formalised in solemn
tones;
And will the Cherubim sing forth for those among us
who
No longer share our Life this hoary, holy hour?

Alas! we do not see the nature of their stay eternal, for
Who can trace the specific nature of that Sleep from the
Cold, sodden turf now traced with flowers and votive
Lamps? That said, we hold to truths since Adam's time
That those who're dead are living still in altered ways

To those we know so well. We know the facts of death,
But not specifics there beyond. For there we falter deep.
And yet we hold to timeless truths and visit those we
Loved in life and loved the deeper still, in Death. Who
Can define, or even trace, the thoughts and feelings of

Us gathered here this bitter morn' together? We draw
Comfort from those thoughts and feelings strong.
Unspoken solace permeates the frosty air at last, and
As we turn to face our Life - together and alone - we
Know that all is done, and have matured this Sacred
Hour.

John Ryan

ALONE (3)

We are left
with our thoughts
- everything else
has vanished.
Stripped like this
is not pleasant.
Until, that is,
we find we cope
alone, and cope
quite well.
Society says we
shouldn't be alone:
necessity demands
we be alone, if
only to confront
our inner selves.
It can be quite
surprising, even
a revelation. The
pain of parting is
amply compensated
for: the joy of
being alone is its
own reward.

AN AUTUMN BURIAL

How we treat the dead
matters:
they depend on our sense
of obligation, of respect.
Though we may have once
depended on them, they
now are at the level of our
humanity.
We choose to accord them
rites and ritual.
They, in their time,
accorded us
love and kindness. For
we are them, they are us.
The autumn leaves and,
later, snowflakes, gently
fall to wrap them in our
love, in their cold repose.
And we adjust, and they
adjust, to a newer form
of life, for this is life
anew, not death, the
flowers and votive-lamps
renew that pact
for now, for e'er.

LOVE IS NOT NEAT

Love is not neat
like a poem;
love is not tidy,
love in the raw
tears at the heart,
leaves the heart
besotted, hungry,
in turmoil. Before
you know it, love
turns gentle,
soothing, full of
the delicacy of silk.
Love, then, even
appears logical.
Even inevitable.
Until the loss.
Berating the
absence, love
in the raw
tears at the heart,
leaves the heart
besotted, hungry,
in unconsolable
turmoil.

YOUR PRESENCE

Everything in life
is coloured by
your presence,
by my having met you
in foreign parts.

Everything in life
would be coloured by
your absence,
were I to lose you
in homely paths.

Frightening:
this cannot be for e'er.

THIRTY YEARS ON

I loved you then, I love you now,
Then was then, I don't know how
We managed all this time,
Without another kiss - a crime.

October's moody, misty rain
Taps gently on the window pane -
My love for you is still the same:
For e'er I'll sing my own refrain.

Times were easy, times were hard,
The odd rebuff, it had us marred:
But we survived, and still we're here
- We laughed a lot and shed a tear.

Undiminished love is me,
Thou matchest all my love for thee;
For e'er we'll be together tied
For I'll always stand right by your side.

DEATH

The trees are flailing about, sensing
The grief of those gathered under:
Nature is in turmoil, as if unsettled
At the loss - the very sandy soil is
Shifting in the wind, all eyes
Concentrated on the unspoken
Wail.

Grief restrained, highlight of this
Drama enacted here and now.
Contrast the dark-suited folk
With the burnished coffin now
Returning to its final spot with
Dignity and awe.

A life of love, the love of Life,
Not extinguished but enhanced
By ritual old and new; the gentle
Mood reflective of the soul now
Entered in the Book of Life for e'er.

LOVE POEM (2)

For I loved you in the morning
and in the night-time, too; for
thirty years we've loved each
other often and with an
intensity known only to us two.

The days they scamper by,
The moon is suddenly upon us,
envious of our love-making:
before we know it, the sun
shines and seals our love.

A FUNERAL

Once you and pouncing about,
Now the fight is o'er;
A complete cycle has taken place -
We are here to witness its close.

Alzheimer's dim, slithering
Advance: never letting go;
Dementia not far off -
It, too, advances slow

And almost imperceptible
To those who're gathered round
But now we say Goodbye today
Upon this sacred ground.

And those who share this sacred hour
Recall the bad times and the good:
This mound recalls another mound
Where once the Mound of Calvary stood.

The birds they twitter on the trees,
The rabbits running wild;
Thou wert our friend in Peace and War
- With the innocence of a child.

HALF PAST TWO

Woken-up at half past two and
go quietly to meet my Muse
downstairs - don't think she'll
turn-up on demand.

My Muse is much more selective:
the gods grant their favours in
much more mysterious ways.
Don't be so mercenary, I tell myself.

The Muses grant their favours one
by one, to whom they will: I don't
want to be rebuffed again. I want
my confidence to grow.

Feels like I'm at the mercy of
mysterious forces, beyond my
comprehension: no moon
shines bright for me this moody hour.

The props the gods provide
have fallen all apart -
but I am not disconsolate
for my Muse is in these parts.

My Muse, that I may know thee
in these wily times:
so I can wax lyrical tonight
and pen thy loving rhymes.

OCTOBER

Leaves scurrying past, their
life-cycle complete, racing
down the street,detached
at last and heading who
knows where, to fulfill a
newer phase of aimless
wandering. Perhaps my
soul can empathise with
them, for they are gathered
up at last, and maybe used
to good.

John Ryan

AN IRISH CEMETERY

Apparently another field,
A field in Ireland, but
Set aside and consecrated,
Blessed, the place where
Loved ones rest for e'er,
Protected by the
Hawthorn bush and trees
Now seen in different light.

Surrounded by the lush and
Fertile land of Ireland, this
Sacred spot does offer
Comfort and a solace rare
To those who visit from
Abroad, a precious time
With loved ones who
Sleep the sleep of Peace.

That we may ne'er forget,
That we may love intensely
Still, 'midst luscious growth
From Ireland's soil - always
Close to heart and soul. The
Body will decay, the Spirit will
Live on 'midst this sacred plot,
and we will come again for sure.

ALONE AGAIN

And I am alone again, creating silence
as an aid to concentration, entering
deep into a conversation with myself.
For I hardly know myself - and
others even less.

Yet, I know silence intimately, for it is
a state of being.

Alone: frowned upon,
but full of creativity. Silence is my
closest friend; serving our mutual
needs we create delightful duets.

And so I'm not alone again.

SALVATION

Maybe now my soul will save itself
This dark, dark night. The world has
Gone to sleep, but I am wide awake
And calling forth mysterious depths
Of consciousness to help me in my
Vigil all alone.

My saving grace is patience almost
Infinite, born of pain almost
Unbearable. My soul is groaning
Deep within: wishing fast
Release it knows will not yet come,
But seeking prematurely a form of
Redemption from my pain
This very Hour.

The gods, though kind, are not so
Kind to such as souls like me.
The gods make no exceptions when
Souls come pleading inner torment,
Even when the choice, it seems,
Is eternity with them. Their darkness
Is our light - our darkness is their
Light. My soul it changes night for
Day, and calling forth release is
Simply to confuse the inner self.

This I know, and yet don't know,
Conflicting movements tugging
Deep within: in desperation now
the soul cries out Release! to
No avail.

Again, salvation is deferred: I'm
Left to face the darker pain alone.

PLEA TO A DEAD SISTER

I'd give anything to have you back,
Dear, dear sister of mine: if only
You could come back for one full
Day. Why, I have all the plans
In place. We'd be just as we used
To be. We'd be happy, and sad
Together, and laughing and
Giggling, too. Oh yes, and
Reflecting and caring and loving.

Please, oh please, come back for
Just one day together. Let us catch
A glimpse from you as to what it's
Like where you are, a unique
Revelation never before achieved.
You'd be able to solve so many
Questions for me and, indeed, for
So many others. You'd tell me
How the other loved ones are
Faring, too.

Oh! Anne, dear, there's
So, so much we could glean from
Each other: please come back for
Just one day - but then, methinks,
Days and such precise
Measurements are not part of your
Present experience.

I'm asking for nothing less than a
Suspension of all the Laws of
Life and Death.

And I know it won't be granted: it
Makes the bond between us so
Much more precious now.

WANDERING SOUL

Negotiating alien spaces in the morning light,
The soul still hungry to understand what drove
Those far-off folk to raise an edifice like this.
The spire to pierce the inner soul, and give
Some meaning here this early, watery hour.
The context full of history's slow detail, we
Wander slowly by and make our exit, only
To confront another packaged bit of what
Was then - and what is now.

By now, the cold has gone and, full of
Fascination, the story's all that matters in
This happy time, for we are in the steamy
Light again, meandering and wandering,
And happy photos too, interspersed with
Coffee breaks, and ignorance dispelled by now.

The soul is questing still for more, hungry
Still for meaning as it questions Who? and
When? and Why? For we are wont to ask
And query yet again, in times when soul
Renews itself, the massive market square,
The inner search for words to feed the soul
In dusty morning light, as alien spaces never
Cease, for we are born to wander here, and
Know these spaces as our own in foreign
Parts.

We leave refreshed and tired, with no more
Time to lose, for what we saw today will be
Renewed the next day, too, in other spaces,
But spaces not so alien by now.

BACK HOME

Returning home is so, so ground-embracing
as to have a sense of deeds well done in
foreign parts. Back to familiar things and
folk who define the very substance of our
ways, and life,

In foreign parts we alter things and folk,
we encounter different ways of doing
their familiar things and meeting their
familiar folk, strangers now becoming
friends.

The very gutteral sounds reminding us of
verbal rhapsodies in time, in tune with
foreign spaces - warm and reassured.

Now back home, we already miss
enclosing warmth, the first encounter
which defined the very substance of the
place we'd chosen as our short-lived
encounter this time round.

Who's to tell what life-enhancing gifts
would flow our way in these beloved
streets of theirs? In response we'd
choose to give a little of ourselves.
And we were them, and they were
us this sharing time, a time of insights
shared and intimacies done, the gifts
so well received, and given, too.

The homely bed it welcomes back,
back home: all is peace and rest
once more.

DUSK TO NIGHT

Hail! the dusk,
precursor of the night,
great is my joy,
my anticipation
of pleasure to come.

Night, the time of silence
and fulsome pleasures
of the mind;
great is my joy.

The mind at its most creative,
the soul, its most solemn,
the spirit, its most vigorous,
the conscious, its cleanest,
great is my joy.

Hail! the hours of moon-lit joy,
holy orb transmitting vibes
to sentient soul, awake,
alive to what it has to offer.
Great is my joy.

SYBIL

I want to know everything,
but what if to no avail?
I want to know enough
to survive my melancholy.
The fascination of knowing
all there is to know: would
I swap it all to be free from
melancholia?

Too close to call . . .Now come
the Muses near to me
this hour of deepest
melancholy. Oh! Sybil, let
me see your cave,
wail no more and
do not rave, for here I
wallow in my lair, I
need you to my life approve.

Cast me out no more, I plead:
instead, I want my case appealed.
Darkened cave for darkened deeds,
take me past the rustic reeds,
where we can play the lyre alone
- my melancholia will by then be gone.

John Ryan

A POLISH GRAVE REVISITED

Apart, yet in the midst of Torun's rush,
sandy soil warmed by late September
sun, the mood is formal but not gloomy,
pottering about to make things tidy for
the long, long sleep of one much loved.
Spare of words, but not of memories,
we stand in solidarity and show respect,
for ne'er we'll see Grandma again.

Votive-lamps flicker flame in light's
sharp rays this gentle, sober morning
hour, heads bowed down, and who's
to tell what private thoughts of
yesteryear unite those gathered
round?

Wild rabbits run, and stop,
and run again, while overhead a lonely
bird recites its warbly dirge in unison
with those who notice not its plaintiff
notes midst silence all around.

And as we leave, the memories are
still too raw for some. For we who
loved thee down the years will love
thee in the years to come, dear
Babcia now at peace.

This stern, sombre hour renews the
aching soul inside, the journey long
now justified, as muffled verbs translate
as happy sounds to match the bird's
altered mood, perched high above.

The grief is grief assuaged this time,
this ritual now complete, and we can
join the rush of Torun's busy whirl
once more.

Torun: a city in northern Poland

John Ryan

ME AND MY PAGE

Me and my page have a strange
relationship. We are wedded to
each other, inseparable, but we
do endure extreme torment.

The page craves attention: being
empty is not natural ti it.

I try so hard to comply - I fail to
satisfy so often. There is a
constant tension, a tightening
of the muscles, until release comes
with a visit from my Muse.

Before that, however, the page is
written-upon, erased, crossed-out,
over and over, so that there is a
non-stop physical battle between the
point of my pen, and the paper.

There is a natural balance, eventually,
between the demands of the page
and my ability to satisfy.

That balance has to be earned.

APRIL

April sunshine, the pleasure of
Sitting in the garden awaiting
Summer's long, long days.

Winter took its toll; begone
With haste. Come the mornings
Bright and sunny - harbinger
Of pleasures still to come.

Easter cannot come too soon,
The May Bank Holidays, first and
Last, entry to summer proper.

April showers, too, to cool our
Ardour and anticipation of
Warmer climes lest we get
Carried away with unrealistic
notions.

April sunshine, bring it on, for we
are cold and want to sit about in
Heat all summer long.

LAMENT (2)

No more words from you
This warm, breezy August
Morn. My soul craves a word:
Just as it used to be
When thoughts of death were
Far removed from discourse
Civilised. Death changed all
That, suddenly. But still I think
That we are one in spirit bound,
Lamenting though I am this sad,
Sad hour.

And yet, my spirit is refreshed
Each time we communicate, for
We were bound in deep, deep
Love, and as the years rolled by
We closer came and then --
The finality of Death.

OLD FRIENDS

I met a friend,
we talked about old times,
it's obvious to me I've changed
to a much more private, poetic
person, these last few years. I'm
not sure that's a compliment -
indeed, I'd say it's problematic.
It shows my age, not my maturity.
And yet - I'm glad I'm me.

All that was then, this is now:
I'm rooted in my own poetic reality,
rejecting so, so much in
favour of a much more private
sensitive way of seeing my reality.

MENTAL DEATH

Alas, no mechanism
in society to enable
me to mourn
the loss
of my Mind.

Grief has assaulted
me, at the very
moment I expected
compassion to
visit, and stay.

The shock of sudden
mental death. The
very trauma
eats my soul alive.

Surrounded by
fellow-inmates in the
Psychiatric Wing, not
one expresses a word
of condolence.

I am
all alone
in
my
grief
-in shock
and
unconsolable.

THE t.v.

I can see the world,
and cut it out of my
life, instantly.
I don't interact,
don't use phone-ins.
It's a one-way traffic,
a mere recipient. My
only input is my t.v.
licence. Because of
my fear of the real
world, I use my t.v.
as a substitute.
I can deceive myself
all I want. I can be of
the world, but apart.
I pay my licence,
ironically, to be
safely isolated. On
my terms.

The real world
cannot be switched off.

FOR WHEN I DIE

For when I die
don't let me lie
alone: in life I
felt alone, but
never really
wanted it so.

For when I die
keep me in your
thoughts: for in
my life I often,
often thought
of you, just you.

For when I die
celebrate my
love of life:
my life of love
for none
but thee.

EMIGRANT

Far away from home I am,
But home is here, there, everywhere;
And in my soul there is a place reserved
For that first home which I thought was
Permanent.

I am an emigrant from that first home:
We are all emigrants from some place on
The planet, even when we draw water
At the universal well to sustain our
Collective emigrations.

Forever re-crossing our home-made Styx,
We always emigrate to new-found mental,
Cultural shores. Each time the cycle starts
Anew, a tapestry of new experience.
The cultural dislocation fades.

For now, we anticipate each new trip,
Adapting well as first response, our
Processes in tune with the deliberate,
Soporific rowing of the oarsman. We are
Part of the fabric of our Underworld,

made for us and of our own making.We
Spin a web, more perfect every time, soon
To be masters of our lot. We welcome
Sons and daughters -- soon they'll too
perfect their trade of supplantation.

John Ryan

I'M THINKING NOW

I'm thinking now of all the times
When I was young and wrote my rhymes,
And everything was happy, bright,
- But it was all to end in fright.

For Life has taught me lessons hard,
Not easy being a wise old bard;
I'm older now and Life is slow,
There's little else I need to know.

Don't get me wrong - I'm happy still,
But happiness is tempered till
We reach a point in Life's hard way
- It's easy, then, to go astray.

To go astray, avoiding pain,
Following the moon's slow wane,
Mistaking fortune for bad ilk,
Mistaking sherry for sour milk.

The human mind is frail and weak:
Composed of cardboard, not of teak;
I need those nerves of steel today -
Lest Life's secrets do betray.

AT THE END

When all the times have come to nought,
And all life's battles were well fought:
Who is to say what might be, now,
Remembering the high and low

Of life's long way, viewed in a blink,
The way it is, or so I think;
That long road's coming to the end,
Life's lovely garden I did tend

With diligence, and loving care,
That garden's brimming - 'twas once bare;
And I am ready to depart,
And from that road I will depart.

And who's to say what will be then,
I do so wish this I could pen
For everyone and all to see,
That on this road I've been true to ME.

TICKLING LEAVES

Two horse-chestnuts perfectly spaced apart,
Edges rubbing against each other,
Outer leaves sensuously tickling each other.
Solidity complements gentility,
Rooted to the ground and a network of
Wooden pipes: the most exquisite leaves
In May-time.

A fleeting glimpse of squirrels jumping
One tree to the other, the rustling
Ceases and all is quiet once more.

The mutual tickling still continues as the
Sudden gentle breeze invites a goodly
Summer hence. Cavorting squirrels know
It's been a long, hard winter since the summer
Last, but they endured and celebrate with an
Acrobatic flourish just for me.

Skeletal no more, the trees have cloaked
Themselves with greenery unique, Nature's
Now awake, but slowly this time round.

SPRING

Mid-May, the sunny scents wafting through my
Garden of delights, the odd bee already
Rumbling along, following its own inner logic.
So much looking forward to high summer, I, too,
Follow my own mental processes.

All the more this time round, given the
Savagery of the long, indeterminate
Winter which wouldn't let go.

The bulky crow lands heavy on the farther
Roof, I sense the twittering of the miniature
Cousins delighting in the new-found greeery,
Bobbing here, bobbing there.

Tea in the warmth of my garden this early in
The year is delight beyond words. Frost: the
Big worry, as I note the delicate tops and
Growing-points of roses soon to display to
Perfection for months on end.

Already I can scent the Muse . . .

MAY SUNSHINE

Bright May sunshine,
So, so luminous,
Deep, sharp May shadows,
Happy, happy May-Day thoughts.

Pitch dark at night,
Blazing brightness in searing
Sunlight, the rhododendron
Giving of its best.

The best of spring now,
The summer near at hand,
The long, enduring winter
Now disbanded.

Twittering among the branches,
Small birds negotiating big
Trees, their delight
Our enchantment.

Long may you stay,
Sweet, delicate, shy May
Sunshine. Sweet May
Sunshine: my content.

I SMELL THE SCENTS OF SPRING

I smell the scents of spring
Just like the bees and delicate
Creatures. I study every detail
In my garden. The south-facing
Fence is teeming and crawling
With the teeniest of teeny-weenies
On a mad, obsessive, seemingly
Illogical, work ethic. How they
Survived the frosts and raw winds
Is beyond me. That was then,
Forever lost. And now is here in
Brilliant sunshine just for me and
All the creepy-crawlies round about.

STRANGE DREAMS

Strange dreams in stranger times
- The afternoon, of all the times.

The sun is burning through
Curtains closed, I am closeted
In my room, barely conscious,
Inhabiting a nether world
Through an unconscious
Dream-like trance.

No effort required,
Yet the effort required is such that
I sweat profusely.

Free of the negativity of the
Psychiatric Unit, I have strange
Dreams, semi-conscious in that
World - the sweltering afternoon,
Of all times.

No logic in my dreams, and yet a
Fully restfulness underneath the
eiderdown while I breathe the
Sleep of peace.

Egyptian cotton - contrast to
Sweltering heat outside,
Oblivious to all except my
Dreams, strange dreams this
Strange afternoon.

SPRING REVIVAL

The blackbirds flit and bob from fence to fence,
The merest glimpse as they land with infinite
Precision. The time of year when we eye all
Nature's ways, the full revival now in place.

There's a sturdiness in the movements
Hereabout, the late May sunshine sets the scene,
The tall, tall tree is shuffling all about,
The wind meditates aloud in the chimney.

The wood is so supple, the noise is the wind
Filtering through newly-born leaves. And I am
Alone with my thoughts. The tree is happy and
dancing, having gained my total attention.

The early flowers burst forth in a madness
Unique, the rhododendron past its best - already.
The breeze in the face mixed with sunshine
Supreme makes this a special time for me in the
Cycle of life.

I love it.

John Ryan

BANK HOLIDAY IN THE GARDEN

A fine tilth giving immense pleasure,
A Bank Holiday in the garden planting,
Busy Lizzies, rhododendrons, Geraniums,
- And a whole lot more.
Roots of all sizes and conditions, the
Sheer smell of soil, a perfect medium.
My back gives sharp bursts of pain as I
Bend slowly, and stand upright again.
Grow-bags for tomatoes, we've been
Here before, and know what will be
A few months' hence. Time of
Anticipation, time of crucial judgement,
Hoping all will be as all should be.

SPRING SHOWER

Yesterday's delights in my garden
Are no more: a gentle rain greets a new week.
An army of umbrellas meandering the High
Road, but this is small fry.
None of the monsoon bursts in other
Foreign fields.
Heavier drops beneath the trees, drip, drip,
Drop, drop: Nature at her gentlest -
Almost apologetic. Summer yet to come,
And show her best.

LOVE POEM (3)

In troubled times and happy times,
Times future and just now,
We will hold each other's hands
And declare a loving vow,
To keep the good times near
Declaring sweet-nothings
And shed a tear, if need be
- Just to be as one.

JULY

Swallows' acrobatics high above,
Sweltering July days, the scents of roses;
Last January we could only dream of
Such delights. No need to travel far
To gain the sun - simply doze right here.
In the garden, everywhere, Nature is
Spilling over: time for my outdoor siesta.
Who wants to sleep when roses smell
As sweet as here? A myriad creatures
Scampering around in my garden of
Delights.

John Ryan

AND I WOULD LOVE TO KNOW THE TIMES

And I would love to know the times
When you are down, depressed and more;
For then we could relate to save destruction
Needlessly: friendly friends, not destructive
Ones. Prosperous survival needs a goodly friend
This hour. This very minute. For I am low
And bowed this very hour, but - as always -
I do know the happy times will reappear
In time, to suit the gods. Happy then I'll be,
If only just to please the gods, and Muses, too.
Come, my friend, and let us be a mutual source
Of light, of strength.

FADED CHARMS

And I would love to tell the tale,
A full life lived, but slowing down,
Enduring faded charms of character.
Love's still there, as strong as e'er,
Arthritis sings its wailing tone of pain
Endured so long as to be the norm.

A deepening sense of Death ahead,
So many have already greeted Death
In youth, and so far I've been spared;
Happily I bear the pain of well-worn limbs
Mis-shapen now and gasping for a newer
Lease of life - to no avail.

The pain I bear each morn', and night,
Endurance is a way of life, a minute
Nearer each time round is Death to me.
But I do not despair. A life full lived
Prevents such negatives,
And love's still there, blossoming
All the time, giving more than ever now.

John Ryan

THE COLD MORN' WIND

The cold morn' wind chisels at my heart,
For I am older now, and colder now,
Somewhat moody and disconsolate.

It never used to be like that,
I used to welcome first the feisty, even
Bitter cold, and bear the breeze
With relish.

But now an older, wizened face
Wants covering-up, a grumpy
Face this very morn', much as I
Would like to have it otherwise.

Perhaps a wiser, older age is creeping-up,
And imperceptibly has stored for
Future use the tell-tell signs that
Third Age so becomes.

Alas! my Youth is spent
Long, long ago . . .

BROODING

The ice-cream man in the distance,
His jingle blown in the soft, very gentle wind:
I brood on my situation, and the jingle ceases
As quietly as it began, and all the time I stand
At my front gate, watching the world go by.

Back comes the gentle jingle, further, far away,
And I'm still here all alone at my front gate,
Brooding silently at my fate in Life, my fate.

And I am brooding on a poem in the making,
Strangers thinking: "What an odd bod standing
there outside" , but they know not what intense
Brooding comes to be, in time . . .

John Ryan

SOME RURAL IDYLL

Some rural idyll in my mind persists
And I am here alone pondering what
Might have been; what might have been
'Midst rural enclaves ancient and unspoilt.

Surviving cityscapes and city life, yet
Yearning for a quieter rural idyll where
I could trace Man's progress with
Precision fine, a Claude Lorraine
Landscape in the background.

And when I alk the city streets,
I think incessantly of greener paths
Which lead to grassy bowers where
Woodbine flowers, yet these are memories
From days of Youth, adieu, adieu . . .

AN OLDER TALE

For I am older now,
Arthritis takes its toll;
I think of days when none of this
Entered upon my soul.

Some days I hardly cannot walk,
My walking stick's my friend:
Yet I am graced with fortitude
Until the very end.

Fascination with the world
Has never been away,
That's why I'm happy in my soul:
I'll never go astray.

Not now in these, my latter years,
The door is still ajar:
My poetry, it keeps me free
My mind, it wanders far.

Let me be free, arthritis gone,
Let me be free this hour
And call upon the Muse today,
And enter her lone bower.

LOOKING BACK

Looking back, remembering a childhood now long gone,
Looking forward, Death staring me in the face,
And I am all alone this hour, yet full of happy memories.

From sixty years ago, I am ready now to go where all
dead
Souls do go, with goodly grace, accepting inevitabilities
When and where they come. But where? and when?

Looking forward now, but I prefer the looking back, the
Vivid memories of youngish days where continuous
Present
Represented then my sense of Time unlimited.

And lo! I do recall what seems a rural idyll, basked in
sunshine,
Midst myriad of flowers and fulsome growth. This was
unending
Summertime: even snowytime a fascinating change that

Disappeared too soon. And now experience provokes
Unsettling thoughts: Death stares me in the face again.
Yet
I am not unsettled: looking back has put perspective

Where and when it's needed most.

DEEP IN THE GLADE

Deep in the glade where wild things grow
I lay on my back and think of what might have been.
I lay alone 'midst the smell of summer's growth.

I look straight up and see the tall trees swaying to and
fro.
The soothing orchestra of sound enters deep within.
I lay alone 'midst nature's song of summer, a myriad

Leaves in unison and all is full of sound, yet peaceful
To the end. This is, indeed, what might have been for
e'er:
It will not last, for soon, too soon, the sound

Will change, extremes of wind and the thud of falling
Leaves, each one changing hue until it sways its way:
Autumn then, a noble Rite of Passage, until winter

Strips it all away, exposing naked bark. Deep in the
glade
where wild things grew, now the winter
Winds and snowy times complete a cycle one more
time.

John Ryan

A PASSING POEM IN THE WIND

A passing poem
in the wind,
 many poems
in the gale,
one long poem
in the calm.

Poetry is
everywhere,
poetry
embraces all.

A spider's web
escapes it not:
death-machine,
source of
endless wonder.

A sticky poem
in itself.

AND I WOULD WRITE

And I would write the kind of poems
that stimulate
yet fulminate
about the loss of
innocence and cleanliness
in nature's ways, due to our
wayward glance at oil-spills
and the rest of it these days.

For I'm confused at climate change,
disenchanted at that wayward glance
we give as recompense.

For I am all alone, and insignificant
in the face of nature's ways.
And I would write again this early
hour to celebrate my input to a
resurrected set of ways, when
concentration and deep study
give a sense of worthiness, at least.

A POEM

A poem is a little gem
that brightens up my day,
a poem in the making
- it's all that I can say.

Composing one small poem
is like a slow, slow snail:
it creeps along my mind at night
and so I have my tale.

A simple poem is goodly stuff,
a force for good in all,
I tell my tale in humbleness
- Creation before the Fall.

Originality I give,
the spider's web complete,
and now I give it to the world
to shimmer, be a treat.

OH! TO BE IN WONDERLAND

Oh! to be in wonderland,
that inner state of calm
and concentration new
this early morn'.
The owl's eyes
penetrate the darkness
deep within, unsettling
momentarily.

This inner wonderland
connecting with the
early dawn, this after
deep, deep sleep
and wiping cobwebs
from the eyes in
pursuit of mental
pastures, damp
with dew.

That very watery
world confuses thoughts
- the street lamps suddenly
switch off,and startle.
Now I can see the world
for what it really is and
in my garden I can see
close-up the waving filigree
of spider's web, its night-shift
now complete.

And oh! in wonderland are favours
to be had but for a little
concentration in the wild,
yet tamed, city-space that I call
my own.

John Ryan

ONE MORE LINE IS ALL I NEED

One more line is all I need
to write, to satisfy that inner urge;
I fool myself that one more line
will tell it all, pithy, grasping all
the meanings possible.

But now is not the time for
verbal wonders: it's the
middle of the night and I'm
tired of weighing, balancing
untidy bits of words
and phrases, fooling
myself further in hope of
being more comprehensible
at last.

Tiredness takes its toll: all
that's left are bitty bits,
depression settles in, like fog,
this poem is just a ragged thing
that won't be fixed
by one more line . . .

READING IN THE EARLY HOURS

Reading in the early hours
brings nourishment galore;
it sets me up for another day,
my mental breakfast all complete.
Years of practice, dawn by dawn,
makes virtue good in company
of gods who favour those who
read. My Muse is present in
these early hours: ah! my Muse,
my Muse, next to me and
comforting, inspiring me to
pen such words as please the gods
after I have been inspired by
voracious reading at my desk
this cold, cold morn'.

HAPPY SUMMER DAYSS ARE GONE

Oh! sweet and sweet,
Oh! happy, happy summer days
now evaporating to a pace that's less intense,
for now September's clouds, cold and damp,
are grey and cover all the sky.
My moods - they're cold and damp,
they, too, are grey
and cover all my mind.
Happy summer days are gone.
No more the roamin' in my garden
at ann early hour, examining the petals
and smelling intense scents from roses
waking-up.

Still we'll keep the memory fresh
in soul and mind through winter's
rugged days and nights.
Happy summer days are gone.

TOO MANY BIRDS

Too many birds lined up
to fly away, one would think;
too few to create an etherial choir.
I change my mind once they chirp
in unison. All summer they flew
in acrobatic harmony, now - one
last time - they fly away to
warmer climes. 'Till their return,
we have a winter harsh to kill,
empty skies for company:
too few birds.

John Ryan

OH! TO SEE MY GERANIUMS GROW

Oh! to see my geraniums grow
to such perfection: pure delight
this summer's day.
The raindrop on the petal makes
me smile once more, my
garden's bursting full after
recent season's rain.
Sturdy though it is, yet so
delicate and full of subtlety.
Luminous in sunshine,
brightness still in rain, it makes
me stare and stare again this
blessed summer day.

DEATH WILL BRING A TRIUMPH RARE

Death will bring a triumph rare, unique
to me: a triumph over life's
vicissitudes and struggles all this time.
And as the acid rain dissolves so much
it falls upon, so death will decompose
my flesh and leave my soul to rest.
I'm confident, convinced, that all is
well in death, it's inconceivable that
death ends all for good. There must be
recompense for actions bearing
positives, just as then and there
account be paid for evil perpetrated
to our kind.
Death will bring a triumph rare, unique
to me: a triumph earned well.

CAN I ASK ONE MORE TIME

Can I ask one more time
if we can sail the spheres
together like we did before?
My Muse, I loved that time
and loved that gift from thee:
grant me one more time this
cherished gift of thine and
we will music make to serve
the gods this special hour.
And while we probe the music
of these spheres, we will
for e'er entwine, promote
our friendship and sing
and sing and sing again
in utter, sheer delight.

I WAIT AND PAUSE

I wait and pause this happy day:
today my poems arrive.
The waiting is unbearable,
for I want to cradle my book
and cuddle my book, and
smell the paper newly-bound.
I wait and pause with
infinite patience:
anticipating pleasures
now to come in bundles of
immense mental joy.
The book is on its way, now
buffeted and pushed around;
but soon we'll be united,
assured I am of chunks of
wisdom forever etched in
every page for all time.
The pleasure is to come,
all mine this day and for e'er.

I AM OLDER NOW

I am older now,
but not too old
to read and write:
to read and write
ferociously at dawn,
at noon, and before
the day has laid itself
to rest.

Sure, I miss the trails
of youth, the green
roads, valleys and the
waterfalls when I was
fit enough to slake my
thirst at the opening of
the limpid pool.

Now I cannot bend that
far, alas. But I have
mem'ries fond:
I am older now.

THE EARLY - MORNING BIRD

The early-morning bird will never
really know how much it takes from
us in terms of light and space.
The early-morning bird I noticed
straight away, swerving,diving,
ascending again: only to repeat
the process with tighter
perfection. We are envious,
rightly so. This performance is
temporary, a few months' time
the bird will be a continent away.
Next year it will return to repeat
these solo ballets all over again.

My beautiful early-morning bird.

John Ryan

THE CANDLE IS MY SOLACE NOW

The candle is my solace now,
candles here and candles there:
muted colours roundabout,
flickering existence at my very touch.
The shock reverting through
my being: Rembrandt comes to mind
this medieval night.

Solace, warm and comforting,
reverting to a time when
mankind needed oil
much more than we do now.
And yet, a sense of comforting,
an affirmation of our
humaneness.

The candle is my solace now.

THOUGH I AM OLDER NOW

Though I am older now,
my time is not so spent as
to call it wasted.
I read so much and
write even more
and life is good and full of
joy and intellectual quest.

Though I am older now,
I have great joy at the
prospect of lesser time
ahead, for each minute is
full of quest, joy and
happiness.

GIVING THANKS

Giving thanks for all the graces
we receive when old:
so often we forgot
when in the flush of youth.
worn body, tired-out mind,
makes me think inevitables.
Worn body, sober mind,
makes me think of
all those things which
go to make a peaceful soul.
And peaceful soul is all I want
at this stage in my life,
avoiding pain and stress
in this older age.

STARING AT THE SKY

Staring at the sky
wondering, wondering
at what might be:
day-dreaming in the
August sunlight.
Making-up words
and phrases for my
next poem.
Obsessed, obsessed
this golden hour.
Bits of words, and
whole new words.
Busy as the bee,
scampering from
word to word,
ceaselessly
meandering, still
staring at the sky.
Masticating
all the while.

SLOWLY NOW

Slowly now, compared to
earlier times,
I make my way in life,
stick in hand.
A shock to realise
decrepit ways may yet
become the norm.
A shock to realise
athletic ways
are to be no more.
Death itself is not
a million miles away:
A sobering thought,
but not one to
frighten me this early
morning hour.
Ye gods, that we may
know our fate,
maximising Life's
few chances so
as to face this Death
in peaceful guise.

LATE SUMMER AFTERNOON

I lazily lounge at my front door,
distracted by the slightest sound,
September sun spreading itself
all over.

Yesterday's wind has blown itself
out: tomorrow's sunshine has
already come to share its abundancce.
Indian summer.

The roses are on fire with gold
and every colour, shade and hue.
This late, late summer sunshine
wishing well to all, and all too well.

ONE LAST SURGE

The roses give one last surge of growth,
before the autumn frosts will cast a spell;
etherial blooms, a final floral mix, as if
for me alone this time. The evenings
darken earlier, a stronger sense of
boundaries being redefined.
These roses please the gods in the
hallow of the summertime, who
could fail to recommend their scent
and colours all? Adieu this time, until
next year: delights that we may find
in time to come, more glorious than
this summer fading fast.

PAST PASSION

For we were deep in love that time,
The world seemed contained
- Yet even then we knew it couldn't last:
The world was too constrained
For the likes of you and me.
But loved we did and loved again
For sure the world
Contained too little love, we thought,
In certainty and innocence.
Oh! love of my life! just one caress was
What the world contained that sensual hour.

THE LEAF

The imprint
of the leaf
upon the softer
mud beneath;
soft-fossilised
for passing pleasure
- and passing
- it will be.

The next shower
will wipe it clean.

MADONNA AND CHILD

A Christmas Meditation

Holy Madonna, I am at your feet,
Outside it's freezing and full of sleet,
Inside I'm burning mad to touch the
New-born Child.
Noli me tangere? Surely not . . .
He was born to save those who
Cannot save themselves, and who
Like Plath have nine lives. Nine
Deaths I had, did I offend you,
My dear Madonna, by ignoring
The niceties of poetry, such is my
Desire to rush to touch and gently
Kiss that face crowned with thorns
A few years hence . . .
Blood at birth, blood at death, Holy
Madonna, and blood of mine freely
Flowing through my veins, in lonely
Search of sanity. The sharp cuts to
Give relief, not to cause pain, and
Still I kneel and want to caress the
Child, - bloodied or not.
Holy Jesu, glaring deep within my
Psyche, grant me sanity, bloodied
An' all, I too, like those who knelt
In the snow at Canossa, would
Gladly kneel and beg a new-born
Child for a lesser-bloodied sanity
So I could fully love the life that's
Lived without the suicidal threat . . .
Pious Jesu, life would be so
Different were sanity to be the norm,
Holy Madonna, forget the stops and
Commas, the rules of Poesy, and
Give thy ear to screams within, which

John Ryan

Plead to Thee for bloodless pulses
And caresses for the Child, the Child.
Sacred Jesu, Sacred Child, let me
Kiss thee warm and kind for I am in
The death-throes far outside in snow
So deep, kneeling not's an option now
For I want to know the breath of cow
And animals that crowd around to warm
A freezing crib with breath so regular
And deep in peace. Holy Jesu, do not
Sleep, see the efforts and the fears, see
The output of humanity, and let me see
Thee close-up and warmed by hugs from
Me. Madonna, Mother mine, hold me in
Your gaze just a moment yet, I do not
Want to die and do not want to fret
In this Mystic time. Holy Madonna, let
The stars shine and twinkle just in praise
Of Holy Christmas Jesu, full of powers to
Give such as me the gift of proper sanity.
I plead, I beg, I do the impossible and go
On my arthritic knees to gaze into the eyes
Of Holy Jesu, mystic Child indeed, and as
You lift Him up for me the better to dissolve
A kiss upon that sacred cheek, I shed a tear
And cry this Holy Time with Kings as witness
To my fading faith, the faith of one whose life
Is racked by intimations of another soul within,
A soul hell-bent on breaking ranks and seething
With insanity, explaining stays in psychiatric
Wings for efforts to try exorcising devils deep
Within the soul. No sweet Muses swirling round
Granting mystic gifts of eloquence - instead,
The dreaded Voices in the head instructing one
To Do it, Do it without cease, indeed without the
Godly gentleness emanating from the Jesu here
Heated by the straw and blankets fit for kings, who
Have arrived from far to see my sight and add their

Breath of love to mine. Privileged indeed I am this
Cold and bitter frosty night, the Star of Bethlehem
A compass for insanity to eek its scabrous way
And leave the Mind alone. Jesu, Jesu, three
Times Jesu I beseech that norms of mental
Instability be erased from minds like mine, so
Prone to inner Crucifixion . . .
Cherubim and Seraphim and choirs of angels sweet
and mild in unison, I add my smoky croaky voice this
Hour in praise: Laudemus, laudemus, laudemus.
Holy Jesu, give me deep inside the kind of peace
That we all crave for us and our loved ones, Holy
Jesu, may the coming year bring those attributes
Signified by Gold, Frankincense, and Myrrh. That I
May know the Way, and see a happy road ahead,
And if be granted gifts from Muses close, and dance
With Faeries, Faery dragons no, but goodly, happy
Kindly Faeries in the midnight bower with whom I
Cavort from time to time, to sing and rhyme and play
A-plentiful in happy playgrounds livened still with
Muses scented sweet, bestowing eloquence upon
Those sodden souls who crave a gift to play for gods
Above. Sweet, sweet Jesu, accuse me not of
Sacrilege, for in my puny way I try to learn Mankind's
Ways to nightly goings-on, deep in shady glade, while
All the while ignoring insane thoughts which are there
Within the brain . . .
Madonna, Mother, Mystic Maid, I plead with thee to let
Me have the graces you can give to those who want to
Know the better powers such that mental torture be no
More. Jesu, Jesu three times Jesu sweet and here for
Us, I go again on painful knee and cry out openly in
pain,
Such is my discomfiture, and plead, and plead again,
three
Times plead thou little Child to listen still to me, though
Countless billions through the Ages have merely asked
What I now ask: Grant us Peace, Grant us Peace,

Grant us Peace . . .
For with hindsight I do know that Blood will flow from
Soft and rosy cheeks as now I closer draw, and smell
The sweet smell of the Infant born, shed not a drop in
vain,
Give me full release from mental torture - the kind I
know
So well. Look upon the tortured souls in mental
institutions
- The ones I came to know so well during my
   incarcerations
And I ask a Final Peace for those who didn't survive . . .
Madonna, Mother Mary, listen close to me in kneeling
agony
And give me some such love as you did have for Jesu
Child.
For I am bad, not mad, Precious Christmas Jesu Child,
help
Me see the newly-born Dawn of Humanity with newly-
minted
Eyes and soul, make me new and make me bold, in
search
Of a perception close to goodly ways, and exorcise my
latent
Mental bent from devils deep within. I carry scars of
torture
Deep, not knowing when the battle will commence for
this
My mind so precious now to me and Thee, and Thee
and me.
Another Christmas meditation coming to a close, this
time
With threat of doing something so, so bad that life would
cease

As life has been down through the years . . .
Sweet, sweet Jesu Child, grant me Peace. Surviving all
the
Months ahead is all that matters now, keep me safe
from
Underworld thoughts, I want escape from crossings of
the Styx,
And sign-up with the ranks of those who in the past year
Showed me kindness, deep respect and a modicum of
love.
Jesus Christus, that I may show the same this year
ahead . . .

John Ryan

DECEMBER SNOW

The world has grown a skin of lethal ice,
My garden's full of snow, never did it
Look as beautiful as now in its pristine
Suit, ready for Christmas. The skin of
Ice is deadly, a no-man's-land. I may
Gaze, but dare not enter this suddenly
Foreign field of white. And yet, beneath
It all, are bulbs bursting with vigour, but
Will not show themselves for months yet.
Fascinating to notice the melted snow
Round the edges of my beloved pots,
the warmer temperature inside each
Pot overcoming bitter cold winds from
The East. Compacted snow is frozen
Over and as I venture out onto the street
I delight in crunching my way forward
Through a wonderland of white, the snow
Is dry and powdery, not the usual sleety,
Wet stuff. It will remain for quite some
Time this time round. The chestnut
Trees across the way look exquisite with
Snow glued-on to every branch at angles
That are dazzling to behold. The pigeons
And the crows and the smaller birds are
Fidgeting and bobbing all about, darting
Beaks into the frozen road: instinct or
Desperation, I ask myself . A blackbird,
Dipping into the waterfont, now frozen
Over: dressed in clerical black, silhouetted
Against the pristine snow. The robin
Redbreast rests reluctantly upon a
Clearing branch, and my winter
Wonderland is now complete.

CHRISTMAS EVE

Waiting, waiting all this time,
Waiting for the bells to chime
To tell me "It's ok to cheer"
- Ignore the smart ones who do leer:
Just celebrate and have my beer.

Waiting, waiting like a child:
Me? Why I'm so meek and mild;
Waiting for the Christmas Bells,
Christmas presents on the shelves.

If only I could be a child,
And have a manner half as mild;
And wait for Santa still to come,
Leaving for him a tot of rum.

Please, dear Santa, come to me,
All the children you can see;
Please make sure I get my gift,
As through all the gifts you sift.

The pail of water has ice on top,
The cat knows this and will not hop
On top to drink - the birds will land
And peck as in a pile of sand.

The garden, too, is full of ice,
Walking there is playing with dice;
I've fallen there this afternoon,
Now I attend to my new-found wound.

Oh! Christmas time, Christmas time,
The time of year when people rhyme
To be together full of cheer,
And what a way to end the year!

John Ryan

A child I am not anymore,
But still I have great hopes in store,
That Santa will not me forego,
Christmas Angels high and low.

Thank you, Santa, you are my friend,
Christmas Greetings to you I send;
I've been a good codger all the year,
I deserve my share of Yuletide cheer.

Three cheers for Santa, that's my claim,
I'm not one to seek out fame,
My stocking's hanging by the fire,
Praising Santa I'll never tire.

Codgers like me are two a penny,
Already I'm drunk - pass me a Renny
Finding it hard to type, you see,
Happy Easter, full of cheer.

Please tell me what they find so amusing,
I may be drunk, but I've not been accusing
So how come everyone's laughing at me,
My head it is reeling: I'll have some black tea.

Black tea and Rennies, a good solution,
It's a bit too late for my Lenten resolution,
But Santa will look after codgers like me,
As I open my presents during afternoon tea.

Oh! Christmas time is Santa time,
One more beer and a glass of wine,
Celebrate the Man for he is Risen,
Evil from the world he now has driven.

Arcadia

I am not exactly a saintly theologian,
I prefer a tune on my melodion.
I'll be damned if I can stand the noise,
I've fallen over and lost my poise.

I'm really pissed and falling all over,
I wish I might land on a bed of clover,
I've landed all right and hit my head,
Happy Easter everyone - I'm off to bed.

John Ryan

MONOCHROME GREY

Grey, grey sky, white, white snow,
Glassy packed ice underneath,
Warily we wind our way and still we slip
And perform acrobatics in the attempt
To walk with a modicum of dignity.
Seven days to create the world, and
It might all have been so different: a
Multi-coloured sky, perhaps? Seems
Like a rushed job to me . . .

At last the weak, watery sun penetrates,
Blue sky follows, I have intimations of
What might have been.

The pigeons, gratified to see so far, are
Flying high: nothing on the frozen ground
For them. Not even Christmas Shelters,
Like we have for humans in this arctic
Avalanche.

The sun it soon evaporates,
Back to a dense, even soupier grey
- And cold to match., snow-clouds
Scurrying past. One by one, and in
Pairs, the birds fly off to God knows
Where: where do they find shelter
From medieval conditions? And then
It's pitch black outside on Christmas
Eve . . .

THE THAW SETS IN

The small birds, in their tens, are scattered
all over the horse-chestnut trees and
performing a twittering extravaganza, in
sheer delight upon the arrival of the great
thaw at last. No more starvation rations,
no more pecking for mere survival.

The lone pigeon sits atop, bemused.
And so do I stand, equally bemused.
It's as if spring had suddenly arrived
this Christmas week - the very stones,
denuded of their coat of frozen snow,
no longer silent, are sharing in the
celebrations with New Year upon us.

Beads and droplets of dew all over the
Japanese Acer, each one a joy to study,
each one a marvel, a whole world, in
itself. A thousand such beads hanging
from the washing line: everywhere is
damp, and happily so, for now we can
walk normally, without slipping and sliding.
Oh! to walk just normally again . . .

NEW YEAR

The stream it bubbles on, gathering so much snow
as to become a fine specimen of a brook, downstream.
And upstream, the rivulet tries to gather as much light
and oxygen to get it on its way. Bend down to the snow-
covered bank, you can hear its signature tune, a rare
few notes of optimism in bleak mid-winter.

Curious that Mankind chose to start a New Year, not
on the first day of spring, but caught deep in snowy
traps when winter's merely half-way done. Were it the
former, perhaps we simply wouldn't survive the long,
long march of doom to April 1st, such is our need for
light, and lots of it. The odd few days of pure blue sky
are merely intimations of what will be, come spring and
summer - ye gods, that we may gain some
nourishment from yon bubbly stream and all it
represents, both actually and symbolically.

On the very verge of the old year, I look for every
possible reason to be optimistic as the New rushes
forth just like my favourite brook. Optimism is survival,
has its own song from deep, deep within the human
spirit. Roll on, roll on, my favourite brook, and sing
your song of innocence, meandering o'er pebbles
fast, negotiating a line of least resistance. Pure,
unpolluted, limpid water from the bowels of Mother
Earth.

New-born rivulet welcomes-in the new-born year . . .

COMPLEXITIES

There are many mysteries to solve,
But none as deep as thee, and I have
Lived, and loved thee down the years
Altogether besotted by thee for
Whatever reasons I dare give this
Lovely, and loving, hour. Romancing
And dancing in celebration of our love
This merry time: being merry, not
Miserable, is the one idea keeping us
Together. Come, let's be merry, dance
The New Year in, and cherish this
Romance of ours.

John Ryan

THE ROCKERY

The miniature flowers survive between the rocks
Of all shapes and shades and sizes, prosper from
Close attention: just enough solid, sun-deprived
Soil, deep, deep beneath. They positively prosper
Now, they've come full circle, and make a perfect
Photo as I wade through a mass of summer's
Offerings by my winter fireside, when all is
Smeared by deep, deep drifts of drowning snow.

The stones evaporate the passing rain, miniature
Petals, a rare, deep red, calling nature's millipedes
To come and browse and watch the show put on.
The larger stones compete for space, jostling
Smaller pebbles: the very texture of one stone
Setting-off the sweet-smelling flower that would
Be crushed to bits. Instead the flower is cosseted,
Protected by the stone - providing shade from
Summer's blinding midday sun.

And I can marvel at the schist, the course-grained
Surface contrasting with the feel of petal on my
Probing fingers now. Nature's miracle abandoned
Soon as summer showers instantly alter patterns,
Colours and shades of multi-coloured miniatures,
Right before my eye. Thank the gods for stones,
Pebbles and flowers in abundance putting-on a
Show for all the world to share, yet how many do
Pass-by and never notice ?

FESTIVE TIME

Pomegranate fills my nostrils,
From my scented candle, I am

Spruced and shiny for the
New Year, all is deadly quiet

As the Big Thaw makes it
Possible to walk again to buy

My fags nearby. Sunday morning,
I've done my bit for the Infant,

And I ruin it all by polluting my
Space with smoke, in spite

Of my patches. Presents given
And received, New Year seen-in,

And I scent my candle full one
More time. And yet, nothing

Compares to my scented roses
In high summer, the scent wafting

Through my nostrils in my garden
Of delights. Ye gods, that we may

Bruise our way through mid-winter
Gloom and deadly silence to the

Higher meadows of mid-summer
When all is happy and delightful

Even where the woodbine grows.
Scents complemented by the

Gushing waters of a trout-filled
Stream, and I am lazy-happy with

My fag. Ye gods, ye gods . . .

MANIC DEPRESSION

They used to call it manic depression,
now bipolar something or other.
Like waking-up and discovering snow,
it accumulates, and by the end it's
a massive, all-encompassing mist, a
fog in the mind that envelops all one's
postures.

Not a problem in itself, except that
yesterday it was one of elation,
wandering the sunny uplands of the
mind, now in the depths of self-
uselessness: utter worthlessness.

My Muse she frowns on me, the happy
faeries have deserted me, I am one of
a kind alone, oh! gods, oh! gods, why
me, why me?

Of all that's known in Medicine, nothing
can help me this cold, clammy hour.

I need to wash: I am permeated by this
contaminating mode of existential
nothingness. Yet a shower will merely
exacerbate things, the roots, the very
watery molecules, will bore
their way into mental crevices unknown
even to myself.

How I wish the faeries would now come
in hordes and take me to their sun-lit
happylands to play the lyre, amuse my
Muse and all will be supreme, but no,
no, no; now's a time to wallow in my
very own lair, lick my wounds and see
this storm out, silent and malevolent . . .

John Ryan

LONGING

In mid-winter gloom, I long for summer days
when all is happy, mild and better for the
health than clammy, misty weather such as
we endure.

Longing, longing, meditating, waiting for the
faintest glimpse of omens rare. Spring will
come, they say, it will be on time, they say,
but when?

Rivulets of snow-melt are all I see in East
Finchley: Nature's mystic wonders are all
enclosed within my books galore, and the
cityscape looks tired, in need of warmed
sunshine in my bare garden.

Longing, longing, waiting still, wait we will
while deciding battles of the elements will
force the winter grip to finally give-way . . .

DAILY WALK

As I wander through East Finchley
I cast a seasoned eye on folk busy
with their routines. I love my little
bit of London Town, and after my
breakdown feel free to meander
where the squirrels pop about,
into Cherry Tree Woods and
further to Highgate Wood.

I sniff the air, and, post- New Year,
feel the faintest hint of spring -
yet far, far away, too far for
immediate relief.

The suburban crawl along the
High Road is measured, almost
leisurely.

My favourite trees are gaunt right
Now, wary folk wear winter warmth.
At surface level, as the 263
meanders past, half empty, all
is set for a fine, modest spring,
hopefully just weeks away. With
my walking-stick for comfort, I
have a lone coffee and watch
the world being busy at being
busy, and wander home to
where the real pleasures are . . .

As I arrive home, the cheekiest
robin redbreast you ever saw,
bobbing about and welcoming
me back to Park Road and my
home pleasures.

John Ryan

My garden, to the casual glance,
is devoid of anything to delight:
Roses pruned, potted plants
pointedly complacent and infinitely
patient for the burst of growth in
spring, is a model of circumspection.

My walk has achieved its objectives.

www.ingramcontent.com/pod-product-compliance
Lightning Source LLC
Chambersburg PA
CBHW021158010426
R18062100001B/R180621PG41931CBX00017B/29